There is only one exit that leads to an expected end

Jennifer Muthoni

Kingdom Publishers

The Exit
There is only one exit that leads to an expected end.
Copyright© Jennifer Muthoni

All rights reserved. No part of this book may be reproduced in any form by photocopying or any electronic or mechanical means, including information storage or retrieval systems, without permission in writing from both the copyright owner and the publisher of the book. The right of Jennifer Muthoni to be identified as the author of this work has been asserted by her in accordance with the Copyright, Designs and Patents Act 1988 and any subsequent amendments thereto.
A catalogue record for this book is available from the British Library.

All Scripture Quotations have been taken from the New International Version and the King James Version of the Bible.

ISBN: 978-1-911697-29-9
1st Edition by Kingdom Publishers
Kingdom Publishers
London, UK.

You can purchase copies of this book from any leading bookstore or email contact@kingdompublishers.co.uk

Dedication

I would like to dedicate this book to all who will read and believe in the only true God and to the believers who wait faithfully for his return.

Many thanks to the Kingdom publishers for their dedication in making the book complete.

Introduction

I remember when I was young, naive, immature, lost and without purpose, I made many poor decisions.

Later in the prime of my life, Jesus found me and came into my life, and he gave me a new beginning with a different perspective. Whenever I need to make decisions now, I depend on him for the direction and outcome because he will keep me on course; 'Not to lean on my own understanding'.

It is every human being desire to survive and therefore our decisions are made on the basis of survival. When we submit our lives to God, we don't live any longer just to survive but we thrive and that is what this book is all about. God involves us in his business here in the earth he created and gives us assignments. Whatever we do great or small, if we do it for the Lord, it is a noble assignment.

He inspired me to write what you will read in this book. Then it is right to call it the assignment he gave me to share with you my reader, what is written in this book so that we be aware what time it is. When we want to know what time, it is, we always have a way of knowing. Either by looking at the clock, or asking someone and in many other ways. Let me be someone who has been given an assignment to tell you what time it is that we are in as God's created people.

It is time for us who are called by his name to live in the fear of him (God) and him alone. God looks at our hearts, that inner attitude of submission in reverence and awe in every area of our lives. Now is the time for check list.

It is time for the lost to know their savior. Without God we are lost and yet we might be in high positions successful and with no worry in life and very settled. Sometimes the circumstances that come into our lives, become the catalyst to awaken us from our comfortable positions. They make us aware that we need a savior.

The corona virus will be that catalyst to stir all of us who are called by the name of the Lord to be people who fear God not the virus. Also, a catalyst to make us aware that the savior we need is Jesus for he is the hope of the world.

Table of Contents

Dedication   iii
Introduction   v

CHAPTER 1: A Decision nobody can ever regret   1
CHAPTER 2: The Deserted City   5
CHAPTER 3: Undivided Attention   9
CHAPTER 4: The Dream   13
CHAPTER 5: Move From the Crowd   25
CHAPTER 6: A Call to Arise.   33
CHAPTER 7: An Invitation   45

Other Reference Scriptures   51

CHAPTER ONE

A Decision nobody can ever regret

Years have gone by and yet that day is still very vivid in my mind. A day that I woke up one morning and I made a life changing decision to follow Jesus. I did not understand what that meant or entailed. I will not write the details that led me to that decision, neither the ups and downs through the years of that journey at the moment. Hopefully one day I will write another book on that story of who I am because of the decision I made that morning.

We are constantly making decisions and I would say that making decisions is a way of life. No matter how big or minor our plans might be, it always involves making a decision. Some are trivial matters; some are important than others and some shape our lives.

Events that occur in our lives, demand that we take action. We have to do something and most of the time whatever decision we make, affects our life for good or otherwise.

The oxford dictionary defines decision as 'a choice or judgment made after considering something.'

Following the outbreak of Coronavirus, the Government announced a lockdown. A decision that was made for the welfare of the people.

Few hours later a friend of mine decided to go and do her usual shopping unaware of what was happening. She immediately called me when she was back in the house. Her aim was to alert me of what she had seen at the supermarket and how necessary it was for me to do my shopping.

The rush for buying was on, people streamed to the supermarkets. There was panic and confusion as people bought extra stuff for storage.

After giving me all the details of what was happening, I told her I did not think it was that serious. I informed her I would stick to my usual way of shopping and hopefully all will be back to normal soon. Little did I know then that it was not what I thought. The normal I spoke about was far-off and not what I anticipated. Today as I write this book the reality of Covid 19 has proved to me how wrong I was.

The following morning the Lord woke me up early at 5a.m and clearly, I heard what he said. It is hard to believe that the God Almighty would be concerned about minor details of my life such as shopping.

With time I have come to understand, why he desires a personal relationship with each one of us. He is our Father and he has a special place in his heart for each child who would dare to know and call him Father. His love and concern for us is unfathomable.

After he awakened me up, he said, 'go and do your shopping for this thing; 'Covid 19' is not going to end as you are thinking'. In other words, my thoughts were too shallow I expected it to last for a few days and not more than weeks. God knew all the details even how it came, what was going to happen and how it would end. He however made it clear to me of two outcomes it would bring.

1. Restore back the fear of God to his Church (the Ecclesia).
2. Bring back the lost to their savior Jesus Christ.

The eternal God had seen the Corona Virus coming and was in control, he has always been and will forever be. For me and may be many others we had expected it to be just here for a few days. That is our finite nature. But God knows all things and that is our hope that we are secure in him no matter what life throws at us.

I pray that the savior of your soul (Jesus Christ) will use this book, to touch your heart so that you will make the only decision that counts concerning your future. I am fully convinced it is the only decision that no-one ever regrets. I have heard people me included who express that they wish they had known Jesus earlier but not vice- versa.

CHAPTER TWO

The Deserted City

The lockdown had now begun and the Government had put the rules and regulations in effect to protect all the people Nationally. We were now hemmed inside the four walls of our homes. It looked very bleak but I could still take a walk to the park and that alone to me was a silver lining in the cloud.

Although there were some restrictions attached to the rules, for me anything was welcome. I was glad just to be out of the house for a while though we were not allowed to linger in the park. Since it was during summer time, I felt the virus had robbed from me one of my precious gifts; the sunshine.

I had nothing I could do to change that, neither the Government. I had to keep reminding myself that God was in control not the pandemic.

When Sunday came and I could not gather with God's family as we always do, I realized the virus had robbed us more than we could count. That is when reality of the deadly virus sunk in.

Let me now tell you about the deserted city. Just a few weeks into lockdown as I was passing through the shopping center, I became aware of the silence. It was dead quiet and there was no soul in sight. There was no activity, no life, every shop was shut.

I did not hear the cooing of the doves, nor the merriment of the people, or the bustle and hustle of the usual daily happenings. Some years past, I watched a Christian movie called 'left behind' and here I was, looking at something similar. But I was glad that this city was not deserted because I had been left behind.

Covid 19 had hemmed all the people in their houses leaving the city in desolation. I couldn't help to think that it will be like that one day in the future. Not only will some be left behind but the earth will be deserted.

I felt a tear running down my cheeks. I felt strongly that I was not getting emotional. I knew it had to do with God's concern for the many souls of men, women, boys and girls that were lost. Many who were not aware of his love and how he longs for them with a passion. How he desires that no one will be left behind. At that very moment he quickened my spirit to awaken me too, to be concerned of the same than ever before. To be concerned that you my reader, will not be left behind.

When Jesus was here on earth, he looked at people and had compassion on them (Matthew 15:32). In our current situation, I knew that he was deeply concerned, because he knew the damage the virus was going to cause to people's life. The one who knows the future and his heart was moved with compassion. That gave me such an assurance and comfort, that despite what was going on and whatever would happen, there was a sure hope.

As I walked back to my house from the park I knew even if the situation was so hopeless God was in our midst. Looking from a human point of view all I could see was a hopeless state and a deserted city. I made a decision to use the eyes of faith and see differently.

The Bible says;

> *"The virgin will be with a child and will give birth to a son and they will call him Immanuel- which means God with us"* Matthew 1:25

Under the circumstances we were in; whether out there in the deserted city or inside our four walls, 'God Immanuel' was in our midst.

He is with us forever. In difficulty times and good times. In the insignificant things and the significant.

In small and big details of our lives;

When we are awake or asleep,

In the dark where we cannot see, he is the light in the darkness even light for the darkness inside us.

In the path where we cannot see the next step; he is the lamp unto our feet.

I can go on and on but if you are called by his name, you know it to be so, and in times like these all we can do is to remind one another of that truth. In addition, we also have the assurance from his word and from the Holy Spirit who lives in every believer. Here is a reminder from that word of truth;

> *"When the earth and its people quake, it is I who hold its pillars firm"* Psalm75:3.

He is the God of all even to those who do not love or acknowledge him. He does not show favoritism. He loves us all with an everlasting love, even when we refuse to make a decision to love him, he still loves and cares for us. He will keep us safe and secure.

Our very existence even in the current circumstances is in his love and power alone. We are firmly safe in his power. He is the 'I AM' (Exodus 3:14) and he holds our lives and the universe in his hands.

As I end this chapter, I hope you have been stirred to reflect on the two outcomes regarding the virus. It is my hope that your reflection will lead you to do something. An opportunity to make a life changing decision.

We will do our part to obey the rules and regulations that the government has put in place. As we observe and maintain good hygiene and keeping our distance, our God will do the impossible. He will bring the pandemic to an end.

CHAPTER THREE

Undivided Attention

As days and weeks turned into months of lockdown, the virus was taking its toll in many ways.

Human beings are social being and that is the DNA of who we are. As many places of social gatherings were shut down, many of us were made aware of how important relationships are. Hemmed in, with no way of keeping contact, even with the members of our extended families.

Months strolled by, and though patience is a virtue, I was not doing very well. It is also the fruit of the Holy Spirit. I must confess that as a child of God, I would have failed miserably if there were any merits being given. I think this was the perfect testing of my patience.

Every month that passed by I kept thinking surely the virus should come to an end now. Remember what I said earlier how the Lord had said to me that it was not coming to an end according to my thinking. But I had not learnt my lesson and I realized that my impatience was fueled by my thoughts and my imaginations.

I had to do something, I therefore decided to cast down every imagination and to wait upon the Lord.

God made me aware that lockdown should be an opportunity for us to give him an undivided attention.

A time to seek him as we spend time in his presence.

Spending time reading his word and in worship.

Spending time in personal prayer and for others.

It was clear to me that what the enemy meant for evil, God was going to use it for our good. Long before the enemy plans evil, a plan of escape is always in place. 'It is finished' that is what Jesus said (John 19:30). It is not what we see around us but what was accomplished over two thousand years ago. There is a plan of escape made possible in any circumstance that comes in our lives.

The enemy had thought that he had destroyed the gathering of the believers in church buildings. Unknown to him, it turned out that he had no power over the airwaves. Just like when Jesus died, it appeared like a finality with no hope for mankind but Jesus is alive forever more.

The devil always fails in his plans and that should be very encouraging to every born-again child of God. Knowing and understanding that through Jesus there is always a way out in any situation because he destroyed every work of the devil.

We continued to have fellowship every Sunday and other church activities through online connection. Through technology God's people were unhindered. God's kingdom has been and forever will advance no matter the opposition until the end when he returns, and that is our blessed assurance.

I started noticing the good unfolding every day in my life and I made the choice to give God my undivided attention. I decided to stop thinking how long the pandemic would last. After all it was just guess work and assumption. God was inviting me to more than I could imagine and therefore I resolved to keep my focus on him.

They say that the choices we make good or bad shape our lives. If we make good choices, it is obvious that good will be the outcome. If we make bad choices then the opposite of good will be the outcome.

Though that may be true, sometimes we can make good choices and things still go wrong. That is because of the evil forces in this world that fight against us. As long as we belong to God, we are not under compulsion of making choices as per the world's rationality. As for the forces of evil against us, we have the word as our defense and we also know that we are hidden in Christ.

God made the best choice for us and we can rest assured that in him we are safe. According to his word we are reminded that to choose his instructions is a choice that is certain no matter what happens.

> *"Now choose life so that you and your children may live, and that you may love the Lord your God, listen to his voice and hold fast to him. For the Lord is your life" Deuteronomy 30:19b-20.*

> *"Choose my instructions instead of silver, knowledge rather than choice gold for wisdom is more precious than rubies." Proverbs 8:10-11.*

When we choose God, according to the above scriptures we have chosen life. As I made up my mind to spend time in God's presence, I realized later that it was the best thing that ever happened in my relationship with God. That is what we miss due to our busy lives. If only we knew that being in God's presence should be a lifestyle we would never again wait to be prompted by the misfortunes of life.

There is no price tug I can put on it and I would never neglect to find time to sit at his feet ever again. God's intention when he adopted us as his, was that we would dwell in his presence forever. To enjoy undivided, unbroken and uninterrupted relationship with him.

Jesus expressed it in a very wonderful and profound way and said;

> *"If anyone loves me, he will obey my teaching. My Father will love him and we will come to him and make our home with him"* John 14:23.

God the Father, God the Son, God the Holy Spirit making a home with us.

As months passed by, the effects of the virus could be felt by all, whether direct or indirectly. There was much suffering, sadness and sorrow as many of our loved one's lives were cut short by the virus. Nevertheless, our living hope had also made it possible for us to find comfort in him. If we are willing to love and obey his teaching, he comes and inhabits our lives.

The God who loved the whole world and died on our behalf desires not only to give us the eternal life but also to make a home with us in this life. When we allow him to dwell in us as he shares in our sorrows and pain, then it becomes bearable. When we are bereaved, he comforts and embraces us in his loving arms.

Remember to choose him for if you do, you choose life.

CHAPTER FOUR

The Dream

People express their desires of what they want to become some day in the future and they call that desire; a dream. It goes like this' I would like to be a pilot, a teacher one day or when I grow up' the list is endless. But that is not the kind of dream I want us to share about in this chapter.

From a Biblical point of view a dream is a night vision or rather it is a divine dream. A visitation from the Almighty God, who speaks to his children in various ways. Sadly, one of the most neglected and overlooked form of communication by his children is through dreams. The very special people he chose as his own and chooses to make himself known in astounding ways.

I would say it is the best method, because it is uninterrupted and very intimate. Too often however, many of us just ignore and not pay any attention. We eventually shrug it off and don't think much about it.

It might be helpful to note that both the new and the old Testaments have recorded several accounts of God speaking to his people through dreams. We all know that he is the same yesterday today and forever. As he spoke through dreams in the past, he still speaks even today because divine dreams are relevant. Hearing the voice of God is paramount.

I must confess I haven't been very keen on that method of communication, for many reasons. But whenever he chooses to give me a dream, it leaves me intrigued especially when he reveals the meaning.

God's desire is for us to have an intimate relationship with him which is cultivated through our love, honor, trust and obedience to him. Such a relationship always leaves us in awe and wonder of who he is and of his ways which are too high. Because they are too high, whether we understand or not should not be our concern but rather that he wishes to commune with us.

I realized we can miss out enjoying awesome encounters with God, if we pick and choose or if we are all the times analyzing. Jesus said the secrets of the kingdom of God or the mysteries of heaven have been revealed to his own and not to everybody (Matthew 13:11) what a privilege and honor? We must remember just like he spoke in parables whilst he was here on earth, even now he has not changed.

Before I write the details of the dream I had, I would like to explore a few examples of dreams from the Bible. The few examples might give us a new insight regarding divine dreams.

Joseph was given a dream by God concerning his purpose or rather his destiny (Genesis 37:5-11). He understood that one day he would have a position of leadership and authority. Several years later it all happened exactly just as God had spoken to him in the night visions.

Sometimes God speaks to us in dreams to give us direction. If he is our guide, he will direct us in the ways he chooses for he alone knows what is best for us.

Other times he uses dreams to warn us of danger, so that we are safe. One can be given a dream where God knows they are going to die, so that they can put their life in order. To be right with him our maker who loves us and has good plans for every person in this world.

One such a person was the Baker; he was an official to the king of Egypt (Genesis 40). He was in prison at the same time with Joseph. The Bible does not tell us the nature of the crime he had committed but states that he had offended the king. One night he had a dream.

The dream was very frightening and he did not understand what it meant. The more he thought about it, he was quite disturbed, unsettled and sorrowful. Joseph noted how sad and worried, he appeared and he asked him why he was like that (Genesis 40:6-7).

Unknown to the baker God had given Joseph the gift of interpreting dreams. So, the baker shared the contents of his dream to Joseph and it turned out that the meaning was what was about to happen to him soon. It was a matter of life and death; no wonder, it had caused him such sorrow long before knowing the meaning.

The God who holds our lives and future in his hands had given the baker a dream to warn him of what the king was planning. The king was not going to give him an opportunity for parole but had planned that he should be executed.

Although that was bad news, the good news was that God was speaking to him through the dream of an opportunity to choose a new life that nothing could destroy. A living hope not a wishful thinking.

> *"Praise be to God and Father of our Lord Jesus Christ! In his great mercy he has given us a new birth into a living hope through the resurrection of Jesus Christ from the dead, and into an inheritance that*

*can never perish, spoil or fade-kept in heaven for you"*1st Peter 1:3-4.

Through the dream, God had shown the baker what the kings plan was over his life. On the other hand, God in his infinite mercy and love was willing to give him eternal live. A chance of a new birth into a living hope.

This dream clearly shows two distinct sides to it. On one hand, the baker had no chance or power to change the king's edict. On the other hand, he had a chance to choose life and the execution would only serve as a gateway to his eternal destination.

The day dawned and the baker was executed just as according to the dream interpretation he had been given by Joseph. That dream shows us how God loves us, and his desire that no one should perish. It is also clear that we should never ignore our dreams, but embrace them as God's visitation to us for our good and for his glory.

There is always hope while we are still on this side of eternity. The baker and the thief on the cross are a sure example of the eleventh-hour chance. It is never late as long as we have breath in our lungs to take that offer.

Let me give one example in the New Testament for more clarity that dreams are relevant even today. Joseph and Mary were warned in a dream that baby Jesus was in danger (Matthew 2:13). They Fred to Egypt just as they had been instructed in the dream. King Herod's evil plans were thwarted through that dream because Joseph and Mary acted on it. They did not ignore or doubt, for they understood that even today God still speaks to us through dreams.

I can go on and on but for now all I can do is to encourage you to fan into flame the gift of God that is in you. Don't ignore the night visions.

A word of caution however, is to be aware that the devil likes to duplicate anything God does. Being aware of his schemes helps us to stay safe. If you have nightmares these, come from the devil and that is the difference.

We can also have dreams from another source; our mind due to the activities of the day as the Bible says in (Ecclesiastes 5:3).

If one spends a whole day focused on an issue our subconscious mind will rehearse it at night as a dream. However, we can always pray against nightmares and against our anxious thoughts. When we pray, we will experience sweet sleep (Psalm 127:2) and only leave room for the divine dreams.

Interpretation or rather the meaning of a divine dream comes from God and that keeps us from error. The Holy Spirit gives the interpretation to protect us from error. If we have not received any revelation, then that means the dream was not divine. God can never give us a revelation of that which he has not initiated. His ways are purposeful. Another important point is God's timing. If no revelation is given it is best to write the dream and wait for the appointed time.

In my own personal experience, I have discovered that if a dream is from God, you can never forget it even after several years. Another thing to note is that a dream from God always comes to fulfillment. When God declares a thing, it will happen (Isaiah 46:10-11) It might not always be immediate like the bakers but in accordance to his perfect timing, there is no doubt it will come to pass.

Remember I gave the title of this chapter 'the dream.' Having now given a brief explanation of dreams let me share the nature of my dream with you.

A few weeks before Covid 19, I had a dream. In the dream, I saw many people multitude and multitude in very difficult situations and I was also among them. We were desperate and, in such turmoil, with no way out. Finally, we managed to get out of the situation into a spacious place. I noted all round this place there were many exits.

Whilst I was trying to make sense of what was happening and which way to go, I realized the people had gone. They had gone through those different exits somehow. I stood there looking, not sure of which exit to take. Suddenly at the entrance of one of the exits, I saw a man who motioned me to go to him.

He seemed to be someone who knew me. Presented with these two factors, one that he was calling me and the other was that he knew me. I decided to take that exit. As I started walking towards him, I woke up from my sleep and that was the end of the dream.

As usual I wrote the dream in the morning- in my journal. Since interpretations come from God, I normally commit the dream to the Lord in prayer and leave it to him.

Sometimes he can reveal the meaning immediately or months or even years later. When it takes years, we can forget the dream but God does not because as I said earlier his purposes will surely be fulfilled. The dreams he gives to us are about Jesus the King and his kingdom in heaven and here on earth. When the time is ready for the dream to accomplish his purpose, he reminds us about it so that we can act on it for we are his co-workers.

Though there are times when we might feel the dreams are personal even then we must relate it to the bigger picture; eternity. For every born-again child of God, everything about us, has an eternal significance. Whether it is personal or about others whatever the dream is about concerns the purposes of God. Jesus lives in us and it is in him we live and move and have our being (Acts 17:28).

As the months passed by, one day during the undivided attention I mentioned earlier in the previous chapter, the meaning of the dream was revealed to me.

The difficult situations that we all seemed to be in with no way out, was the pandemic. Coming out into a spacious place, meant that it was going to come to an end. That is good news, that God will bring an end to the virus.

The exits I saw in the dream had two meanings; one of a good outcome and another of a bad outcome. This sounds parallel to the baker's two outcomes of his dream. One was the execution and the good was of an eternal outcome.

The many exits all led to a dead end. The good news however, is that there was one exit where I saw a man who was calling me. The man represents Jesus. That exit was not leading to a dead end like the others. It leads to eternal life and that is the good outcome for all mankind. For with God in control doom and gloom is not the finality. The multitude I saw in the dream, Jesus calls us to take his exit.

> *Jesus said to him, "I am the way, the truth, and the life, no one comes to the Father except through me" John 14:6.*

The Holy Spirit continued to reveal more details of the meaning of the dream and what every exit represents. I will only discuss a few using the following scripture to clarify;

> *"We all, like sheep, have gone astray, each of us has turned to his own way" Isaiah 53:6.*

The danger of our 'own way' that we turn to, becomes an idol which simply means a false god and it is not pleasing to God. Like the many people I saw in the dream, each of us has turned to his own way taking any exit. Let me discuss with us three very common in our day, that the Holy Spirit highlighted to me. Bear in mind the above scripture says 'we all'.

1. Religion- is a set of rules and regulations of traditions practices made by man. A doctrine that is from man which hinders people to worship God in Spirit and Truth and thus becomes an idol.
2. Good works- Sounds appealing to many of us, and makes us believe that we can have our own way of making things right with God.
3. Anything that takes priority in our lives- The list of the things that we give first place in our lives instead of God, those things become an idol. They take the place only God deserves and it does not matter what form or shape, the truth of the matter it is an idol.

There is another danger of going our way and that is why God grieves for us, because it leads to death. Remember that all the exits I saw in the dream, led to a dead end except one. Although, there is no one who likes talking or hearing about death, it is a reality and I wish there is a way I can avoid the subject.

We have all lost someone we love or we know, through the virus. Take comfort in knowing God knows and grieves with you. My heart goes out to you too and I pray you will experience the embrace of God's loving arms. He is the only one who feels and knows our pain and the only One who heals the broken hearted. He is also the only hope beyond the grave.

Remember that death came as a result of the fall but the story did not end there. On a positive note, Jesus died and rose again and is alive forever more. What that means, we too will die and rise again and live forever more. Though we might not understand such a mystery, we can put our faith and trust in God and rest. God loves us with a passionate love and that is why he longs for us to take the exit which leads to where he is. Without him in our lives we have no hope.

Please note and be fully persuaded that the highlight of the above three points is not for condemning or to make us feel guilty. God's purpose for us has always been and will forever be, that we will have the fullness of life. Surely an exit that leads to a dead end is not the fullness of life. Many times, in life, because of our human instinct we are easily tempted to choose what makes sense or is common. In times like this when there is so much confusion and misguided truth, it is better to take the road less traveled. If you care to join me you will have no regrets, because my guide knows the road very well. He is a sure guide to all who choose him.

Many people when they visit other countries for holidays or as tourists, take tour guides whom they have never met or known before; but they still put their trust in them to guide them. We too can put our trust in God to guide us through life because he is our creator and he knows the way.

Days and months have turned into over a year now 'Covid 19 'is still here and we have the Vaccine now. We appreciate and recognize the hard work done by the experts in medical science. A breakthrough like that brings hope and raises our expectations, no wonder then why many are talking about going back to normal.

Though we are all looking forward to that, in the excitement of what appears normal let us remember the virus did not give us a warning it was coming. I don't want to be pessimistic but no one knows what tomorrow might bring. However, we can use the pandemic as a wakeup call and make a decision to choose the right exit. The One who knows about tomorrow, motions us to take that exit. We have no power over our lives but he does, because he created us for a purpose.

I am not in any way trying to frighten you, coerce or put pressure on you. Jesus' love is gentle, pure and genuine with no strings attached and also freely given to all. The decision belongs to every individual.

We all want freedom to choose and that is why many of us choose what we want not what God wants for us. Freedom is a good choice but it depends on the issue.

There is freedom that seems and appears like it is freedom but looking at the results in days, months or years to come we realize that we missed what freedom means. That realization can come when it is too late in many instances.

A simple illustration I can think of is, of food indulgence. If I decided I can eat whatever I want and at any time without a care in the world, in a few years' time the results of my freedom would be detrimental.

Let me give us another illustration; We cannot see the heat from the sun but we know that the sun gives heat, because we feel the effects. We cannot see the wind but it causes effects that make us know it is present.

In the same way we do not see God but the effects of his existence are seen in the transformation he brings in people's lives all over the world. We can deny it and say otherwise but one day we will acknowledge it but we don't have to wait for that day; the time is now. Joseph's brothers denied that they would never bow their knees to him, but years later they did. Similarly, we can also refuse to bow to Jesus now, but one day we will.

One of the traits of our fallen nature is denial. That is the reason why many of us deny God's existence and that he is our creator. But since he knows our simple nature, and because he cares and loves us deeply, he physically revealed himself to us in the person of Jesus Christ.

> *"Who being in very nature God, did not consider equality with God something to be grasped, but made himself nothing, taking the very nature of a servant, being made in human likeness. And being found in appearance as a man, he humbled himself and became obedience to death- even death on the cross."* Philippians 2:6-8.

For the sake of all mankind; God became a man, but many continue to deny that reality which I also did for many years. I have mentioned how the baker was given a dream to make his life right with his maker. Please note that we too like the baker were condemned to die because we also rebelled against the King. Jesus loved us so much and made a decision to take our penalty of death and that is good news and that is why we bow before him in appreciation, adoration and honor.

Many times, I have heard people say they don't want Bible bashing. Believe me I am in total agreement with that, because love is gentle, patient and considerate. God is love, pure love and full of mercy.

Though that is so, like the baker God speaks to us in many ways to make it right with him while there is still time.

It might not be through a dream, for his methods are innumerable, but whatever way he chooses, it is always in love, tailor made and clear. Sometimes we can miss a golden opportunity of a life time if we regard every conversation about God as Bible bashing.

Since the onset of the pandemic, you might have heard this expression every day and in most public places; 'we are in it together'. That means next time anyone tells you about how God loves you, their intention is not to 'Bible bash 'but rather that what God has for us all, that 'we are in it together.'

One final note regarding my dream. Though I am calling it my dream, it was not only about me unlike the bakers, but many people. In conclusive of this chapter, I would say God was speaking to me and to many people including you because you are reading this book. I took my decision to obey and honor God and make right on my part.

Remember in the beginning of this book, I mentioned about two groups of people whose life would take a new direction. To whichever group you belong, you alone have the power to take action, to choose the exit that leads to life.

CHAPTER FIVE

Move From the Crowd

During the Covid period I observed a few things that have negatively affected us. I mentioned earlier in a previous chapter that we are social being, our nature that God created in us. For many months now since the outbreak of the pandemic, our social status has been at stake.

We have become very antisocial out of fear and to follow protective procedures and guidelines. We all know that this of course is nobody's fault. It is important to obey the Government and also protect one another. All we can do is to guard our hearts from being antisocial and not allow the virus to destroy our love for one another.

The very title of this chapter at first glance, may appear to be propagating antisocial behavior. May I suggest that is not so but as you continue reading, you will get the full picture.

In the previous chapter, I wrote about the dream concerning the path mapped out for us. Life is a journey, but there is a specific path that leads to our destination. In the natural world some things are obvious and specific. A simple example I can give is of a train and the rail lines. For a train to get from point A to B, it has to use the rails. Our path to the destination where we are going is only one. We cannot get to our destination in any way or every other way.

To follow that path, it is paramount to move from the crowd. We have all discovered and learnt that someone can be safe from the virus by distancing themselves.

Although distancing from others might not be a great discovery, innovation, or creativity; Nevertheless, discovery is in our DNA. In decades past great discoveries have been made and are still being made.

The one who created the universe gives us the ability to do great things. We might not admit or recognize that to be so but my point is that we can explore and discover great things. Some of us might never explore and discover great places, but we can all explore and discover our lives and that is greater.

What we will explore and discover greater than going to the moon is 'who we are; why we are here; and what happens when we die'? I have nothing against going to the moon but that is the reality.

The reality of discovering beyond the natural as confirmed in (Jeremiah 33:3).

Let's continue with the subject about the crowd and ask ourselves; Could there be any danger of moving with the crowd? Does it really matter?

I will answer these questions with examples of people who moved with the crowd and what was the outcome.

Remember every decision we make in life will always have an outcome.

A story is told of a peasant man and his donkey. Being a very poor man, he decided to sell his donkey. One morning he set off to go to the market with only one goal in mind; to sell his donkey which was his only source of income. He took his son along with him.

Along the route, he came into contact with three groups of people separately. Each group advised him or rather gave him their opinion of how he would get the donkey to the market without wearing himself or his son or the donkey down.

They argued if he took their advice, he would get good value for his donkey. Because he was desperately in need, he thought this was a good advice.

Unfortunately, every group advised him differently and he had to adhere to each group's opinion. Some of the people had good intentions, some made fun of him and ridiculed him.

By the time he came into contact with the last group they had walked quite a distance. They were both weary, tired and hungry and the donkey too. With this last group, there seemed to be too much noise and arguing each person wanting to give their opinion. They mocked and laughed at the old man.

They were certain they were more enlightened than the old man. They ignored and overlooked the wisdom that comes with old age and they took control of the situation. That however did not go well with the donkey. It became very agitated and could not bear the changes any longer.

In the ensuing commotion and confusion, the donkey took to his heel and ran for his life. Gone and disappeared never to be seen again.

When the man got back home that day, he was in a worse state and poorer. He had no peace, only regrets for his actions. It was too late; he had followed the crowd.

A second example is found in the Bible. If you are not aware, the Bible is the manual of our life or call it the map we should carry for our journey. Many of us have heard or read about a man called Noah. Noah was asked by God to build an Ark. Let me mention to you here before I move on, that the creator God is the designer of everything that we see and not see and including us.

We were designed to function according to his plans and requirements therefore, once we are aware of that we can understand how the story of Noah relates to us. It is widely known as 'the story of Noah and the ark.' Known to some as just a nice story or only for Sunday school children. To others an income generating story through movie productions. To the believers it reminds us of the God who designed us and who requires that we serve him in awe and reverence. It helps us also to know that he is in control of the universe and everything in it and he makes right and wise decisions concerning his creation.

There is much more we can get from the story but for this moment, I want to use it to show you the truth and reality that moving with the crowd has devastating effects.

During Noah's time people were not living according to their designed purpose. They all did what they wanted to do according to their heart desires except Noah. God created us to know and worship him. To honor him in high regard and reverence for who he is and to obey everything he commands us to do but that was not so during Noah's time.

> *"Then the Lord saw that the wickedness of man was great in the earth and that every intent of the thoughts of his heart was only evil continually" Genesis 6:5.*

The verses that follow the above scripture expresses how God was grieved by their wickedness. (Genesis 6:6-7). Because God is Holy and the earth belongs to him, he decided to take action. The action he was going to take, was to wipe out all the people that were in the face of the earth.

That action may sound and appear harsh and unfair to those who do not understand the character of God. Careful observation of this account however, are two important points of certainty and assurance that are clear:

One is that although all the people were wicked, Noah had made a decision not to move with the crowd. (Verses 8& 9).

The second point displays God's love and mercy. Though he was grieved, he was willing to reverse the decision he had made, because his mercy and love supersedes judgment. That is why he asked Noah to build an ark. To wipe the people from the face of the earth was not his desire. We were created to oversee everything on earth that God has made, but that was not what they were doing. The people had chosen to do what their heart desired. When people become very corrupt, it affects everything else in creation. The earth also needed to be cleansed. New beginnings for all and everything.

Every day as Noah hammered the nails through the wood, he also told the people of God's mercy and love. He informed them he was building the ark with a capacity to include anyone who was willing not to move with the crowd. Anyone who would choose to believe that they were created by God and that they belonged to him only. Anyone who was willing to receive God's love and mercy not judgement. Anyone who was willing to follow God's way not their own desires.

However instead of anyone accepting the mercy, love and grace of God they mocked and ridiculed Noah. Just like they mocked and ridiculed that poor peasant.

The nature of man- to mock and ridicule for we are sinful from birth and born of Adam. Jesus however was the second Adam and in him we are given a new birth and we become a new creation.

Back to my story of Noah. He continued to build the ark not concerned about all the negative critique around him. He was not deterred and was fully convinced that only one opinion matters; 'God's opinion'. Because he too was concerned of the people and did not want them to be destroyed the insults and ridicule was nothing to him. He was more concerned that they would take seriously what God had to offer them; a second chance and a new beginning. He endured their ridicule and insults for their sake.

When the Ark was finished and Noah entered the ark with his family and all the animals, God's mercy was demonstrated again.

The Bible says God waited for seven days before sealing the door. God's desire to give a chance to anyone who would want to change their mind, but again no one made any move to enter the ark. We know the rest of the story of what happened. The sad ending for those who chose to move with the crowd.

My third example involves, Pilate who was a Roman governor in Judea. He was a man in authority, but despite his position he followed the crowd. His decision to have Jesus put to death was not based on a wise move. He decided to move with the crowd.

The wife's warning not to make a foolish decision fell on deaf ears (Matthew 27:19). He was more concerned about protecting his reputation. I can only speculate that he took that action for future election. Whatever the reason, he chose to please the crowd. He was not like Noah who knew whose vote counted.

Remember in a previous chapter I mentioned that anything we give priority as number one instead of God, according to the principles of heaven, is a god. Pilate decided pleasing people as his highest priority.

What can we learn from all these three examples I have shared about?

1. That God created us as unique individuals capable of making good choices in life and not move by everybody's opinion or expectations. Since he is the one who has got good plans for us, his opinion is the only one that matters.

2. There is a day of reckoning and the designer will come one day to reclaim back what he designed. Like Noah we must live according to our designed purpose and with reverence fear of God.
3. It is also clear that the choices we make in life are very crucial in relation to the end result.

In conclusion to this chapter let us remember that people are still the same as they were during Noah's time. The same during Pilate's time and same as they were towards the poor peasant.

Some people tell us that the world came as a result of a big bang. Others tell us there is no God and others that there are many ways of getting to heaven.

People are changeable and we all know that is our nature. We can say something today and the next day say the very opposite of the same thing. That is what happened with the crowd as they welcomed Jesus. They shouted in excitement and danced for Jesus, laid palm branches and others their cloaks for him like a carpet. It was a very joyous and happy occasion (Matthew 21:1-11).

Some days later the same crowd was shouting but this time in anger, insults and accusations saying 'crucify him, crucify him' (Matthew 27:22-24).

So, before the pandemic ends, for it will end as there is nothing permanent in this world. It will also end because God is in control and powerful. Going by the dream I had, we had all come out of the difficulty circumstances; which means an end.

What will your decision be? To move with the crowd or to make a life changing decision.

God made you a unique being, special and endowed with greatness inside of you. He loves you so much and desires only the best for you. He values every person highly regardless of their color, gender, status or age. Explore and discover that life for yourself, don't be dragged along by the crowd.

Remember the rule for the 'Covid 19' is to keep a distance to be safe. There is a similarity with that rule concerning our eternal outcome; if we are to be safe, we must move from the crowd. Follow the exit with no crowd to keep at a distance and be safe and your future will be certain.

CHAPTER SIX

A Call to Arise

I strongly believe that it is vital for me to emphasize once again, what the Lord spoke to me what would be the pandemic outcome. Not only is it vital but a matter of urgency. The God who turns what the enemy meant for evil into good. To safe you the hustle of looking back to the introductory page, these are the two expected outcomes;

1. To the church of Jesus Christ, the fear of God would be restored.
2. To the lost, that they would turn to God for salvation.

If you are reading this book and you are in the second group, I believe you have read and heard that God loves you. Not only does he love and care for you, but that he has a good plan for you which is to give you a future and a hope.

Whilst you reflect on everything you have read up to this point, it is my prayer and hope that you will respond to the invitation in the next and final chapter of this book. For you who counts yourself in the other group (The Church of Jesus Christ), Jesus Christ is calling us to arise to a certain position. To have the fear of him alone is the position that is unshakable and fully secure. Other fears cause us to hide and we can be distracted from fulfilling what God is calling us to do, yet he is our hiding place.

> *"The Lord Almighty is the one you are to regard as holy, he is the one you are to fear, he is the one you are to dread, and he will be a sanctuary"* Isaiah 8:13.

Since the onset of the pandemic, there seems to be an increase of fear than never before. It might be an error in my observation but there is fear everywhere especially of death. Many people say that it is normal to fear but that is not what the Bible says. The only fear we should have is the fear of God. God desires to use those who are called by his name as vessels of hope to the fearful world. We are the light of the world and that light can be dimmed by fear.

We all know that there are two kingdoms in this world;

One, is the kingdom of God which is of light, love and truth.

The other kingdom is of the devil, which is of darkness, fear and lies.

Since we are not of darkness and we cannot lie then we cannot also be people who are dominated by fear. Though we inherited fear from Adam and Eve, we renounced that inheritance when we accepted Jesus Christ into our lives. When Adam and Eve sinned the reverence fear of God was affected by sin and as a result what took over is fear of anything and everything. They were even afraid of God and had to hide from him yet before that, they had walked with him in a perfect relationship of fear and trembling.

The list of all that we fear is endless but Jesus came and restored back what was lost. Jesus restored us back from being afraid of God and also from any fear. When we are born again, we are translated from the kingdom of darkness, fear and lies from the moment we accept Jesus Christ as our Lord and savior.

We become a new creation immediately but that does not mean that the holy fear of God is automatic or we are freed from fear instantly. Obviously, the exchange takes place in us instantly, but a process begins in us so that we are changed to be a people who fear God and not have any other fears. Though we may attend church, read the Bible, pray heaven on earth prayers, and do many other things we do as Christians regularly and faithfully, only God knows those who fear him. However, he wants to use what the enemy meant for evil- the pandemic as a catalyst to restore his church to its rightful position. To fear God in reverence and honor.

'Do not fear' and 'fear God'; The countless repetition of these words in the Bible is a clear indication of how serious it is to God that we heed that command. May we too as his chosen, loved and set apart people make a decision to respond for the time is now.

Fear had paralyzed and had made me a captive for many years. The grip of it hindered me to enjoy the abundance life that Christ came to give. I used to think there was nothing wrong in having fear. There might be many who are God's children who think the same way. Some say it is only human to have fear. I don't deny that because the issues and challenges of life that bring fear are well founded and real. Fear is real because it comes from the fallen world of the devil and the devil is real. According to (2nd Timothy 1:7) the Bible says fear is a spirit and since it is not from God, the solution is to cast that spirit of fear out of our lives.

If we do not cast it out, with time it becomes a stronghold, but since we all know that Jesus is our stronghold then we must be careful not to allow fear to hold us in any way and must be broken so that we can be free.

When we have a hunger and a desire to please God, the Holy Spirit enables us to grow and mature. We are commanded to find out what pleases the Lord. In finding out we will ask ourselves whether he is pleased when we live in fear and yet he is all powerful. Not only is he powerful, but he is able to change us from glory to glory for that is his desire. The effect will be that the fear of everything that we fear is replaced with the fear of God.

Jesus rescued us from the kingdom dominated by fear, into the kingdom that is unshakable which will endure forever. That is why he commands us and says to us;

> *"I tell you my friends, do not be afraid of those who kill the body and after that can do no more. But I will show you whom you should fear; Fear him who, after the killing of the body, has power to throw you into hell. Yes, I tell you fear him" Luke 12:5.*

I strongly believe that we cannot be effective in advancing the kingdom of God in this dark world if we are not free indeed. If we meditate day and night on the scripture from Isaiah quoted in the beginning of this chapter we need not fear if God is our sanctuary

We thank God for his word because just as he told Joshua that if he meditates on the word day and night, he would be prosperous and successful, he tells us the same too (Joshua 1:8). The word that led me to understand how bound I was by the spirit of fear was the story of Lazarus. I was like Lazarus, delivered from death yet living my Christian life wrapped with the grave clothes of fear. I am very grateful to the Holy Spirit for his truth that he gave me through that word and his power that released me and may that be your portion too.

I became aware that faith and fear cannot co-exist together and that is clearly stated in the words of Jesus to his disciples when he rebuked the storm.

> *But he said to them, "Why are you so fearful? How is it that you have no faith? Mark 4:40.*

Another thing that cannot co-exist with fear is love. Jesus the perfect love lives in us and he casts out all fear. If there is fear in us of other things, people or anything else then we are not made perfect. (1st John 4:18).

To combat any fear, all we need is faith in God and our love for him. The faith of God, not like the one expressed by those in the world. Our faith is sure and certain because it is in God.

We all marvel whenever we read in the Bible about the heroes of faith, how they accomplished mighty, extraordinary and great things. The secret was because they had no fear and by faith, love and obedience to God, they overcame every obstacle.

> *"who through faith subdued kingdoms, worked righteousness, obtained promises, stopped the mouth of lions, quenched the violence of fire, escaped the edge of the sword" Hebrews 11:33-34.*

I would recommend you to read to the end of the chapter and see everything they accomplished.

We too belong to the same God who had commanded them not to fear anything. If we obey God and fear him alone, we have no need to fear anything or anybody in this world. Jesus said it clearly that he came to destroy the works of the devil. No doubt then that the devil's kingdom has no power over us here and now. We also know that ultimately it will come to a complete end.

However, we cannot refute the fact that everyday there are numerous issues in life that do and will come our way, that cause us to fear. Even if they do when we are set free, they have no hold or power over us. we are called to trust and know that nothing can harm us.

We have not been promised a smooth journey, void of the things that bring fear, but we have been promised of God's presence with us. Because we know and understand our God is bigger than anything and that he exists; we should refuse to look at those issues in fear but instead with faith.

Fear undermines the greatness of God. It also makes us disregard the promises of God. One example of a promise we disregard is of death. We have eternal life which is greater than death. So, the promise God has given to us is that death has no power over those who are in Christ.

If we are dominated by the spirit of fear, we can never enjoy the fullness of life as God intended us to. It is also true that one cannot claim to be free indeed if bound by the spirit of fear. I am speaking out of my experience that when I obeyed to renounce and cast out the spirit of fear in Jesus' name, with the help of the Holy Spirit, I was made free.

I made up my mind to live my life by the Spirit of God and choose to trust and to believe in his word. Now whenever I face issues that bring fear or the enemy tempts me to fear, I never give in but always remind myself who I am and to whom I belong. Whatever your fears may be, God is greater and he lives in you (1st John 4:4b).

Since we profess to be victors not victims, or we are more than conquerors and that Christ leads us in triumphal procession, then that is who we truly are. I discovered later when I became free that quoting all those scriptures can be just a mechanical utterance and not living it or the demonstration of it.

The Bible says 'the door the Lord opens no one can shut and the one he shuts no one can open'. It is important to know how the spirit of fear gains access into our lives. In many cases and most of the times, the cause is due to the traumatic issues of our past. Now is the time to let God close that door and you will be healed and free to fear no one and nothing else but God and God alone.

You will henceforth walk and experience victory over the sins that ensnare, over every demonic power, over strongholds and any power of the enemy. You will also experience a greater desire to walk in awe and reverence fear of him who is worthy to be given the highest place.

Currently the enemy has been very busy whispering about death due to the virus. To many in the body of Christ, but we are in crucial times than never before. Fearful times, but as long as we have the fear of God, we are secure in him.

May we choose to live by faith, to fix our eyes on Jesus and to meditate on his word, day and night. Above all, to put on the whole armor of God (Ephesians 6:13-18). Even after we put the whole armor of God, we must not be very comfortable. We are not settlers in this world.

Let me tread here carefully and in love what I am about to say; that heaven is our home. If that is true then even the fear of death, should not keep us bound. We believe what every word that comes from God's mouth says.

> *Jesus said to her," I am the resurrection and the life. He who believes in me will live even though he dies; and whoever lives and believes in me will never die "John 11:25-26.*

Jesus is our example and he had no fear and yet he lived in the same world where the things that make us fear reside. If we are becoming more like him in every way, one of his characters was fearlessness and that is our inheritance.

Let me now shift back to the title of this chapter; 'the call to Arise', but bear in mind the issue of fear as the foundation.

Recall also that I mentioned earlier how God wanted us to give him our undivided attention during the lockdown. I want to share what was the outcome of responding to that call in the next few pages.

I believe we all enjoyed that opportunity of spending undistracted time in the presence of the Lord. I am also sure that we all experienced wonderful and awesome things that God revealed during that time.

It occurred to me how precious we are to him, 'the treasured possession we are to him'. Whatever the Lord might have revealed, think of it, as the best outcome of lockdown. For an encounter with God is everything, there is no better place to be than in his presence.

> *"You have made known to me the path of life; You will fill me with joy in your presence, with eternal pleasures at your right hand" Psalms 16:11.*

For some of us, what he spoke as we sat in his presence, was personal and to be pondered in our hearts. Although sometimes it is personal, there are also times he sends us to share it with others. Many of the people healed by Jesus wanted to follow him, but he would tell them to go back home to their towns and tell others.

His assignments sometimes differ. To his disciples, he said 'go and make other disciples and teach them everything I have taught you'. Subsequently, the same command has been given to all who are called by his name in our day.

God desires that we hear what he says to us. That is why the Bible in Revelation chapters 2 and 3 puts so much emphasis seven times repeatedly;

> *"He who has an ear, let him hear what the Spirit says to the Churches."*

It is my prayer that during the lockdown, you heard what the Spirit was saying to you dearly beloved of the Lord. If it was personal, may you treasure it like Mary in your heart. If it was for the body or the world, may you discern and have the courage to share it without fear.

I believe what the Lord said to me was twofold; personal and also to be shared with you.

I have already shared most of it in the previous chapters and up to this point, but he sealed it with his word in (Isaiah 32:9-20). Since it is a long passage, I would implore you to take a moment here and read these verses for yourself.

The passage mentions the complacent women but I believe it is for all those who are in Christ, male or female, young and old. Those who revere the name of the Lord. Those who pray and desire to see the kingdom of God come to earth as it is in heaven. Those who do God's will and pray for the same in all the earth.

We all know that once we are in Christ Jesus, we are all sons of God because we have the same Spirit of God and are heirs with Jesus; (Romans 8:14). The real use of this word complacent mentioned in that passage (Isaiah 32:9) simply refers to those who are self-satisfied. We are not a people who are only concerned that we are going to heaven. Though that is the best thing we are all looking forward to, it is also important to take others with us. That is the reason I would not think the calling was for the women only. Women however express their emotions more than men and the call is for those who are willing to mourn for the lost. How serious we should be for those perishing and hence do something.

God is calling us all to arise. If you are a born-again child of God with concern for the lost, male, female, young and old. In summary of that scripture;(Isaiah 32: 9-20) we are being called to arise and take action.

'It is time to arise from feeling secure and not be at ease, or be complacent. A time to be troubled, to tremble, strip ourselves bare and hear his voice.'

I understand and hope you do too, that he is not calling us to be troubled or tremble due to our financial situations; neither due to the storms in our lives. Not even due to our daily needs or any other concerns.

'He is calling us to be troubled because of the land overgrown with thorns and briers. To mourn for all the houses of merriment, the wasteland, the desert.'(verse 13)

'We are to continue to do so not just once. As we come out of the place of complacency, feeling secure and at ease; We will mourn, shudder, strip off our clothes, and beat our breast;'

> *"Until the Holy Spirit is poured upon us from on high and the desert until it becomes a fertile field, and the fertile field seems like a forest" Isaiah-32:15.*

Jesus is still seeking the Lost. He wept and died for me and you, that is why he wants us to mourn and be troubled just like he did. Will you respond to his urgent call to prepare his way for his second coming? We are alive at a time as this, the Kairos time, for a purpose. (Kairos time is a Greek word meaning now.)

During his ministry here on earth, Jesus trained, taught equipped his disciples for the advancement of his gospel. He prepared them for his departure and for his return.

We read of their faithful commitment and how they laid their passions and even lives just like their Master. He is our Master too and he is calling us to follow wholeheartedly.

We have been trained taught pruned, prepared and equipped in the same way and for such a time as this, for the same mission. He has healed our wounds and our hearts are flowing with his love and compassion for the lost. It is my prayer there is nothing that will hold us back.

As I end this chapter, join with me in reflecting about the issue of fear. They say where there is learning there has to be a reflection. We cannot fulfil God's call if we have not yet been delivered from the spirit of fear. Whom will you choose to fear; God or all the things that make you fear?

Now is the time to make a decision.

CHAPTER SEVEN

An Invitation

This is my final chapter of this book and it ends with an invitation to you my reader if you have never said yes to Jesus. In the world we live in when we fall in love with someone, we never keep it to ourself. We normally tell them and a relationship begins or in some cases they refuse to accept our love and that means no relationship is formed. Jesus left his heavenly home because he fell in love with us.

Once we accept his love, he writes our names in his book of life. The purpose of this book is to share with you how you can be sure that your name is written in that book of life. If you do not have a personal relationship with Jesus right now, he is inviting you to that personal relationship, as the first step.

> " For God so loved the world that he gave his one and only Son, that whoever believes in him shall not perish but have eternal life" John 3:16.

The world mentioned in the above scripture is every human being on the face of the earth. God loved us so much even to die on our behalf.

We have all witnessed that Covid 19 did not affect any other created thing except the people even our animals. We are unique and precious being, very precious and highly valued by our creator.

The people in the whole world that God so loved and gave up his life for. The people he created in his own image, male and female. We are the one the virus attacked and it has brought much pain, sorrow, suffering, despair and hopelessness. Jesus came and took our place, wore our shoes; of pain, suffering, sorrows, sin and even death. That is enough for anyone to ponder, explore and discover.

Once you desire to ponder, explore and discover for yourself, you will move from believing what the scholars, the philosophers and others tell us about God and the creation. As you ponder, explore and discover since you are' whoever' (see the above scripture), you will know whether you are born again or whether you are a believer. Both of these terminologies have the same meaning.

I would like however to expound who is a believer or born again, according to God's standard and requirements. In the whole world there are many people who say they believe in God. Others claim or say they know God.

However, we are called believers not because we say so. Those who believe and live their lives according to God standards and requirements are 'Born again' John 3:3-8.

The following scripture explains how they become believers or born again.

> "Yet to all who received him, (Jesus) to those who believed in his name, he gave the right to become children of God" John 1:12.

From this scripture it is clear that it is not enough to know about God or to believe in God, but we must also receive him.

We can say, that we know someone but unless we have a personal relationship with that person, then we can't have a right to their heart and we can't say we know them.

All over the world, there are so many people we know just because of their fame but we have no relationship with them. We have never even met them but we claim that we know them. However, we can say we know them but only what we hear or read about them or people tell us about them. We see them and know them because they appear on our TV screens in our homes. We may however, have no personal connections with them and they in turn may have no clue who we are, but we still claim to know them.

To know God is not like that. The right to become a child of God is to receive him in our heart. Once we open the door of our heart and let him in, we can claim we know him. Our relationship is not one sided, he knows us and we know him. He has access to our lives even to be Lord over our life.

The other thing that the above scripture says, on how we have the right to become a child of God; is to believe in his name.

> *"For there is no other name under heaven given to men by which we must be saved" Acts 4:12.*

Salvation is only given by Jesus. He alone, is able to save. We may claim to be very good people and that could be true, but our good works can never qualify us as God's children. If we are to make the most crucial decision of our lifetime, it is only based on receiving him and believing in his name nothing else is acceptable.

Once you become a child of God, it means you have received eternal life. A life that cannot be affected by anything in this world, even death. I have heard many people at the end of their journey in life wishing they had known Jesus earlier than later.

One thing I have never heard is anyone person regret that they know him.

As you choose to follow him daily, you will discover that things begin to make sense.

As you read the manual of your life which is the Bible you begin to understand more of your relationship with God. The Holy Spirit dwells in the heart of every believer and he guides us in all truth as we grow in our relationship with him.

From that moment on, we are never alone to navigate our new found life. The privilege to never walk alone all the days of our lives becomes ours because we are legitimate children of God.

Let me share a few thoughts that are very practical and important but not life giving.

We may have vaccines against every sickness that afflicts human-kind;

We may have all the silver and gold in this world;

We may be well fed, clothed and have no need of anything;

But there is a place in every human heart called eternity; Ecclesiastes 3:11, that only God can fill. That is also why he is the only true God because he is the one who put eternity in our hearts when he created us. He alone loves you and that is why he died for you.

As we come out of this pandemic, he does not want us to look at life as before and say' sera, sera whatever will be will be'. Rather be grateful to be alive but at the same time ask ourselves some hard questions.

Where do you begin you might ask?

Let me give you the answer in closing with a song;

> "*There is a way back to God*
>
> *From the dark paths of sin,*

There is a door that is open and you may go in; at Calvary's cross is where you begin.

There is a fountain filled with blood drawn from Emmanuel's vein. And sinners plugged beneath that flood lose all their guilt stains."

Yes, come to Jesus your savior. His arms are wide open and rest from strive, sorrow and wrong and you will find rest for your soul.

Finally, my prayer is that whether you are a believer or not your heart has been stirred and your mind has been renewed through the scriptures used in this book.

May God put a new song in your heart, to his glory and praise.

Amen!!!!

Other Reference Scriptures

Introduction
Deuteronomy 33:27- The eternal God.
Isaiah 46:10-He knows all things.

Chapter One
Isaiah 2:5, John 8:12, 2nd Corinthians 4:6 – Jesus the light of the world.
Psalm 119:105-The lamp to my feet.
Exodus 3:14, John 8:58, Luke 22:70- The I am.
Romans 8:28- Evil turned into good.

Chapter Two
Hebrews 13:8- Jesus is the same.
Jeremiah 29:11- The good plans.

Chapter Three
Romans 5:12-19, Ephesians 2:1-8, Condemned to die.

Chapter Four

Chapter Five
Luke 10:19- Nothing will harm you.
Isaiah 22:22, Revelation 3:8-The door he opens.
Luke 4:29-30, Mark 12:12, John 2:15- Jesus had no fear.

John 11:44- Lazarus was wrapped.
1st Cor.1:20-The scholar.
John 8:36-Free indeed.
2nd Cor 2:14- Triumph possession.

Chapter Six
Psalm 139:16, Revelation 21:27

www.ingramcontent.com/pod-product-compliance
Lightning Source LLC
Chambersburg PA
CBHW071544080526
44588CB00011B/1788